P9-DCZ-738

FIRST **Bank Account**
AND FIRST **Investments**
SMARTS

Jeri Freedman

To my niece and nephew,
Laura and Matthew Freedman, with love

Published in 2010 by The Rosen Publishing Group, Inc.
29 East 21st Street, New York, NY 10010

Library of Congress Cataloging-in-Publication Data

Freedman, Jeri.
First bank account and first investments smarts / Jeri Freedman.—1st ed.
    p. cm.—(Get smart with your money)
Includes bibliographical references and index.
ISBN-13: 978-1-4358-5270-9 (library binding)
ISBN-13: 978-1-4358-5546-5 (pbk)
ISBN-13: 978-1-4358-5547-2 (6 pack)
1. Bank accounts. 2. Saving and investment. 3. Teenagers—Finance,
Personal. I. Title.
HG1660.A3F74 2010
332.6—dc22

2008040844

Manufactured in the United States of America

CPSIA Compliance Information: Batch #CR010240bYA: For Further Information Contact Rosen Publishing, New York, New York at

1-800-237-9932

Contents

4 Introduction

7 Chapter 1
Bank Accounts

19 Chapter 2
Managing Your Bank Accounts

25 Chapter 3
Investing for a Sound Future

32 Chapter 4
The Basics of Investing

43 Chapter 5
Principles of Sound Investing

55 Glossary

57 For More Information

60 For Further Reading

61 Bibliography

62 Index

Introduction

The key to controlling your financial life is responsibility. As you prepare to take charge of your own life as a young adult, one important area you will have to deal with is finances. How you handle money now will affect how much money you'll have in the future. This, in turn, will affect your ability to do the things you want in the future.

Most people would like to be able to spend all the money they make doing things that they enjoy. They'd like to be able to buy anything they want on the spur of the moment. But spending money continuously without a thought for the future can lead to financial disaster and large amounts of debt.

Saving and investing are important parts of planning for your future. They are ways of increasing your wealth, in addition to working and earning a salary. Furthermore, the sooner you start to invest, the longer your money has to grow and the more money you will eventually have.

The first step in obtaining financial security is to figure out what your long-term financial goals are. Once you are out on your own, you will need to figure out how much money you are earning and what all your expenses are. This process is called budgeting. Making a budget allows you to ensure that the money

Paying for purchases with checks makes it easier to keep track of your spending and helps you budget so you can achieve your long-term goals.

you pay out is less than the money you earn. It also allows you to see how much money is left over after you pay your expenses. You can then decide how much of this money you want to spend and how much you want to save or invest. Budgeting gives you control over your financial future, rather than leaving it to chance.

The same type of analysis and thought will enable you to invest in a sensible way that both allows your money to grow and protects it to the greatest extent possible. This book starts out with a discussion of banking and bank accounts. It then discusses investing both for retirement and to increase your wealth. It describes a variety of investment types and explains how to analyze a stock. It concludes with some general advice for sound investing. Note that this book is intended only to give you an introduction to investing. Before committing money, you may want to talk to an investment professional.

CHAPTER 1

Bank Accounts

The first step in opening a bank account is to decide what type(s) of account(s) you want. The following list explains the most common types of accounts provided by banks:

Checking accounts: The purpose of a checking account is to keep your money in a safe place—the bank—while you use it to pay for short-term expenses. You can take money out of a checking account by writing a check or using an ATM (automatic teller machine) card (also called a check or debit card), as described later in this chapter.

Savings accounts: The purpose of a savings account is to put money away for long-term needs. To encourage you to put money into the bank and leave it there, the bank will pay you interest. Interest is an amount of money equal to some percentage of the money in your account. For example, a bank may

A representative at the bank will assist you in opening an account. He or she will explain the features of the specific accounts the bank offers.

pay 3 percent interest annually (each year) on money in a savings account. If you put $1,000 in this bank, you would earn $30 in interest at the end of one year.

Interest-paying checking accounts: Some banks offer interest-paying checking accounts. You can write checks on these accounts, too, but the bank pays a small amount of interest on the amount (balance) you leave in the bank. The interest rate on interest-paying checking accounts is usually lower than that paid on savings accounts. In addition, you

may be required to keep a certain amount of
money (a minimum balance) in an interest-paying
checking account.

CDs: Many banks offer a type of investment called a
certificate of deposit (CD). When you buy a CD,
you agree to invest your money with the bank for a
specific period of time. The bank, in turn, agrees to
pay you a specific rate of interest on the money you
invest. CDs come in a variety of durations (lengths
of time) and minimum amounts. For example, you
can buy a CD that lasts for six months, one year,
or longer. Usually, the longer the duration of the
CD and the larger the minimum amount you are
required to invest, the higher the interest. CDs
provide a higher return on investment (or profit)
than savings accounts and interest-paying checking
accounts. However, there is usually a penalty fee
that you must pay if you take your money out
before you are supposed to.

Simple and Compound Interest

Interest is money the bank pays you for the use of your money.
There are two types of interest: simple and compound. Simple
interest is just a flat percentage calculated on a sum of money,
called the principal. The money you place in an account or
receive as a loan is the principal. If you put $1,000 in a bank
account, that $1,000 is your principal.

Simple interest is calculated as follows:

Principal × Interest Rate (with the percent converted to
decimal format) = Interest

In this example, where the interest rate is 10 percent, the interest would be:

$1,000 × .10 = $100

You will not often encounter simple interest in banking and investment transactions, however. In most cases, you will be dealing with compound interest. Compound interest is calculated on the principal, plus any interest already received. Thus, every month, the amount of your principal will go up, and the amount of interest you receive will be larger. The point to remember is that compound interest is a very effective way to grow a small amount of money into a much larger sum of money. Every month, the amount on which the interest is based increases. You can find out how much money you will earn from compound interest in a given period of time by using the following formula:

$$V = P(1 + R/F)^{FY}$$

Where:

V = Total value
P = Initial principal
R = Interest rate
F = Frequency (number of times per year interest is calculated)
Y = Number of years

Let's return to our example of $1,000 with an interest rate of 10 percent per year. Compounded monthly (twelve months per year) over a period of five years, this would be:

Protecting Money in Banks

Banks make most of their money from the interest they get on loans they make to people and businesses. Where do they get the money they lend? From people who put money into accounts with the bank. You put money in the bank, and the bank lends that money to other people.

You might worry that if the bank lends people money and they don't pay it back, the bank won't have the money to give you when you try to take your money back out (withdraw it). However, the Federal Deposit Insurance Corporation (FDIC), an agency of the U.S. government, insures any money up to $100,000 that you put in a U.S. bank account. Furthermore, this insurance applies to each bank you deposit money in. So, if you had $100,000 in Bank 1 and $100,000 in Bank 2, your money in both banks would be protected. In 2008, the FDIC temporarily increased the protected amount to $250,000 through December 2009. Be aware that FDIC insurance applies only to money placed in checking accounts, savings accounts, and CDs. Some banks offer investment accounts, such as mutual funds (which are discussed in chapter 4). Money in stock and bond mutual funds is not protected by FDIC insurance. However, reputable brokerage firms carry insurance provided by the Securities Investment Protection Corporation, which protects your investments up to $500,000 if the brokerage firm fails.

$$V = \$1,000(1 + .10/12)^{12 \times 5} =$$
$$V = \$1,000(1 + .0083)^{60} =$$
$$V = \$1,000 \times 1.0083^{60} =$$
$$V = \$1,000 \times 1.64 =$$
$$\$1,640$$

Thus, at the end of five years, you will have earned $1,640. Note that 1.64 is 1.0083 multiplied by itself 60 times. But don't despair—there are many online compound interest calculators that will calculate the interest for you. One online example is www.webmath.com/compinterest.html, or simply go to www. google.com and search for "compound interest calculator."

How to Write a Check

When you open a checking account, the bank will provide you with checks. The diagram on page 13 shows the main parts of a check. It will come printed with your name and address, the name of the bank, and an identifying number indicating which bank the check comes from. At the bottom of the check are two long numbers. The first is a routing number, which identifies the bank that the check comes from. The second number is your account number. These numbers are read by automated systems used by banks for electronically transferring funds.

How to Make a Deposit

Of course, before you can take money out of a bank account, you have to put it in. Putting money into a bank is called making a deposit. If you are depositing a check, for example from a part-time or summer job, you will need to do two things. You must endorse the check and then fill out a deposit

Write name of payee here

Write amount in words here

Write date here

Check number

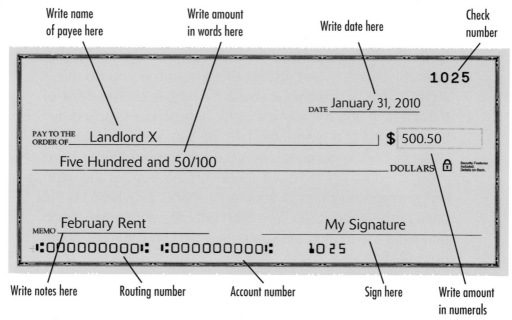

Write notes here

Routing number

Account number

Sign here

Write amount in numerals

When filling in the amounts in numbers and words on the check, start as close to the edge of the line as possible so that no one can add numbers to the amounts.

slip. If you are depositing cash, you will just need to fill out a deposit slip.

To endorse a check, you simply need to sign your name on the back. It is also a good idea to write your account number on the back of the check. (This is especially true if you are depositing the check through an ATM.) You can then hand the check or cash and the deposit slip to a teller or deposit it in an ATM. Deposit slips are usually provided in the back of each book of checks. They are also available at the bank. The following diagram shows a typical deposit slip.

List the amount of each check in the space provided and total them. The line to the left of the check amount is for the identifying number of the bank from which each check comes. This helps the bank's staff identify which deposit a check belongs to, if it becomes separated from the deposit slip. Some people omit this number and just list the amount. If you do this, it's a good idea to write your account number on the back of the check. If you are using a blank deposit slip supplied by the bank instead of a preprinted one, be sure to fill in your name, address, phone number, and account number. If you have more checks than there are spaces on the front of the deposit slip, you can list them in additional spaces provided on the back of the deposit slip. You then total the additional checks and write the total in the space provided on the front of the deposit slip.

Write date here   Write account number here   Write identifying bank number here   Write amount of check here   Write cash amount here

SAVINGS DEPOSIT ☐ Statement ☐ Passbook ☐ Holiday Club

Date _____ Account # _____

Name of Depositor _____

Address _____

_____

BANK

1-800-XXX-XXXX

Checks and other items are received for deposit subject to the provisions of the Uniform Commercial Code or any applicable collection agreement.

CURRENCY		
COIN		
CHECKS (list singly)		
TOTAL DEPOSIT		

⑆0 2 1 20 1 38 3⑆   6 1

Write total here

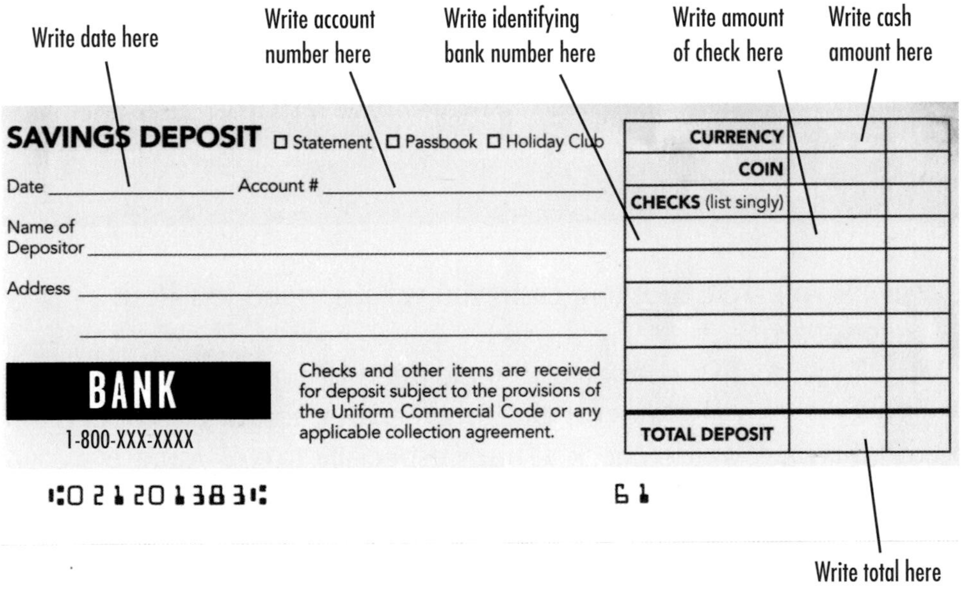

Fill in the information on a savings deposit slip, as shown here. Double-check that you've included all the checks and be sure to endorse the backs of the checks.

ATM Cards

In addition to checks, most banks today provide account holders with an ATM card (also called a check card or debit card) that they can use to access the money in their accounts. When you get an ATM card, you choose a code consisting of several numbers. This is your personal identification number, or PIN. Because anyone who finds out your account number and PIN can take money out of your accounts, never tell anyone your ATM number. And be sure to pick one that's easy for you to remember. You should never write your PIN down and carry it in your purse or wallet, or leave it in your desk where someone can find it.

To use an ATM card, you insert it into a slot on an automatic teller machine and type in your PIN. You will then see a menu that allows you to perform activities like withdrawing money, depositing money, or getting the balance in your account. The balance is the amount of money currently available in your account.

Many stores and restaurants also accept ATM cards. In some cases, you will run the ATM card through a card reader and enter your PIN. In other cases, a cashier will process the transaction the same way that he or she would process a credit card. Either way, the money for the purchase is immediately deducted (subtracted) from your bank account.

Choosing the Right Bank

There are two main factors to consider when choosing a bank: cost and convenience. Most banks charge a fee for using their services. The fee may be a flat monthly charge, such as $8 per month. Or, it may be a per unit fee, such as $.50 for every withdrawal from a savings account. Every bank has a

When using an ATM, be sure to keep others from seeing your PIN, and, for safety, avoid using machines in isolated locations or late at night.

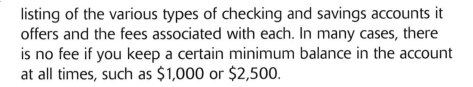

listing of the various types of checking and savings accounts it offers and the fees associated with each. In many cases, there is no fee if you keep a certain minimum balance in the account at all times, such as $1,000 or $2,500.

Do It Direct

"Direct deposit" means that the money due to you is sent electronically directly to the bank, instead of being given to you in a check. This method can be desirable because the money goes immediately into your account on payday, rather than when you manage to get to the bank with your check. Sometimes, there is no fee if you have your paycheck deposited directly into the account. You can also arrange to have payments for bills automatically deducted from your checking account. This is called direct pay.

Before you open a bank account, you should make the rounds of your local banks and obtain a list of the fees and minimum balances for various types of accounts. You can then see which bank has the lowest fees for the amount of money you'll likely be depositing.

First, you must be able to get to the bank easily. So, you will most likely want to choose a bank close to where you live, go to school, or work—or, better yet, one with branches close to all of these places. Second, you may want to choose a bank with conveniently located ATMs so that you can easily access your accounts. You can probably use your ATM card at other banks' ATMs. However, most banks charge a fee ranging from $1 to several dollars if you use an ATM card that doesn't come from that bank.

To open a bank account, you will need to bring to the bank the money for an initial deposit, a photo ID (such as a passport or driver's license), and a Social Security card. If you do not have a passport or driver's license, you can obtain a state-issued photo ID by bringing your birth certificate to your state registry of motor vehicles. A bank representative will then set up the account for you. You must be eighteen years old to open a bank account; if you are younger, your parent or guardian will have to open it for you.

Now that you know how to choose your bank and open your accounts, the next chapter will provide you with information on managing your bank accounts.

CHAPTER 2
Managing Your Bank Accounts

It is very important to keep accurate records of the money you put into and take out of your accounts. In the case of checking accounts, the bank will charge you a large fee if you write a check for more money than you have in your account. This is called bouncing a check. In addition, if you write a check to a company and it bounces, the company will often charge you an additional fee. Therefore, you need to keep track of the checks you write and reconcile, or balance, your checkbook each month.

How to Reconcile Your Checkbook—and Why

Each box of checks that you buy comes with a special notebook called a check register. Every time you write a check or make a deposit, you should note it in the check register.

At the end of each month, you will receive a statement from your bank. A statement is a list of every deposit and withdrawal you made, every check that the bank paid, and any interest the bank has paid you. You can use the statement to verify exactly how much money you have in

Balancing your checkbook every month not only gives you an accurate idea of how much money you have but also helps you catch any errors made by you or the bank.

each account. The verification process is called reconciling or balancing your checkbook. Since it's easy to forget to enter a check in your register, balancing your checkbook is an important way to keep from bouncing checks.

To balance your checkbook, first compare each check, withdrawal, debit card purchase, and deposit listed on the statement with what you have listed in your register. You should check off each item in the register. What you are left with will be checks you have written that the bank has not yet received (outstanding checks). You may also have deposits that you made after the statement was mailed to you. Subtract

Protecting Yourself Against Identity Theft

Identity theft is a fast-growing crime. It is very important that you protect your user name, password, PIN, and account numbers for all your investment and bank accounts. Never write down any of this information on paper or sticky notes. Do not use easily guessable numbers, such as the last four digits of your phone number or your birthday or the name of your dog, as a password. When you get paper statements for your accounts, bills, and offers for new credit cards, do not throw these in the trash. Instead, get a small shredder and shred them before throwing them out. Many banks and investment firms offer an "e-mail only" option for state-ments. If you have regular access to a computer, you may choose to use this option.

Inexpensive shredders are available at any office supply store. Crosscut shredders offer the best security by making it impossible to reassemble the strips of paper.

any outstanding checks from the ending balance total on the statement. Add any additional deposits. This will give you an accurate total of how much money you actually have in your account. Update this number in your check register if necessary.

Managing Your Account Online

Most banks today allow you to manage your account over the Internet. To do so, go to your bank's Web site and look for an area on the home page that says something like "Online Banking." There should be a link there that says "Enroll" or "Register." When you click that link, you will be asked to provide information like your account number and a user name and password. Once you have enrolled, you will be able to log in with your user name and password. There are many functions you can perform online, such as checking the trans-actions that have taken place in your account. You can see the deposits, withdrawals, and interest payments. You may also be able to transfer money from one of your accounts to another, update your address information, get copies of statements, make payments for credit cards or loans you have with the bank, stop payment on a check, and order checks. In some cases, banks offer additional online tools like a checkbook balancer, which you can use to reconcile your checkbook. In addition, some banks offer similar mobile banking services for people who can browse the Web over an iPhone, BlackBerry, or similar handheld device.

Do not keep passwords, PINs, or account numbers on your computer. Computers are easy to steal, and hackers are always trying to find new ways to read the data on your computer's hard drive. Do not leave your browser open with any bank or investment-related screens open. Casual passers-by can easily

k of America Online Ba...

nk of America ≡

Home · Locations · Contact Us · Help · Sign I

Search

ine Banking ▶ En Español

view
In
ll Now
t You Need To Enroll
t You Can Do
le Banking
ne Banking Demo
ne Banking User Guide
ne Banking Credit Card
 Drive
Pass
ne Banking Guarantee
ice Agreement
d Reviews
uently Asked
stions

mation for New York.
ge state

u know you can Sign In
ur Home page?

"I don't see how anyone can live without it!!!"
— KellyfromNC ★★★★★

See what people are saying about
Online Banking from Bank of America

Learn More

America's premier Online Banking service
It's free. It's easy. It's secure.

Get started with Online Banking today.

Enroll Now

- Don't wait for your statement to arrive in the mail. View and track your accounts anytime.
- Forgot to send a birthday gift? Transfer money fast to friends and family from your computer.
- Life is hectic. When you're on the go, receive account alerts via e-mail or mobile device.
- View up-to-the minute credit card account activity, pay your bill online and more.
- Save time and postage when you pay bills online. It is fast, easy and free.

Still undecided? Learn more. View Demo Read Customer Reviews

Bank of America's industry-leading safety features give you greater peace of mind

- Learn more about our award-winning security features like SiteKey and SafePass, and how they help protect you.
- Lower your risk of identity theft and mail fraud by viewing copies of your checks online and stopping delivery of your paper statements.
- Get a special offer on industry-leading security from Symantec, only from Bank of America: Free 90-day introductory subscription.

This is an enrollment home page for Bank of America (http://www.bankofamerica.com/onlinebanking). When you click "Enroll Now," the system will walk you through the steps to set up online access to your accounts.

gain access to your accounts if you do. Most browsers—including those on cell phones and personal digital assistants (PDAs), such as Palm and BlackBerry pocket computers—allow users to back up page by page. For this reason, you should always close the browser completely when you've been viewing one of your accounts, especially on cell phones and PDAs, which are easily lost.

In addition to online tools provided by banks, there are also a number of software programs that you can purchase to manage your finances. The most well-known software for this purpose is Quicken. Such software provides you with an online check register, but it goes further. It provides the ability to keep track of your investments. It automatically downloads information from your bank and investment account. In addition, it provides you with the ability to create a variety of reports, including budgets, reports that show you what you've spent your money on, and reports that tell you how your investments are doing.

Chapter 3

Investing for a Sound Future

The first question that probably occurs to you is: Why invest at all? This chapter focuses on the two major reasons for investment: retirement and increasing your wealth.

Investing for Retirement

One of the most important things you can do financially is invest for retirement. You might think, "I'm very young. Why should I worry about retirement when I get my first job? I can do that when I get older." The answer is that, as with savings accounts, the longer your money is making a profit, the more you get from compounding. There are two main types of accounts used for retirement investing: 401(k) plans and individual retirement accounts (IRAs).

401(k) Plans

The 401(k) plan takes its name from the section of the tax code that describes it. A company sets up a 401(k) plan for its employees. Employees can contribute up to a certain percentage of their salary, for example, 15 percent. In most

The Retirement Planning Store

Plan
to
Retire
Early...

Come in
and See
How.

Investing for retirement when young works: $10,000 invested at age twenty earning 5 percent annual interest will be almost $100,000 at age sixty-five; at 7 percent annual interest, it would be more than $200,000.

cases, the company will match, dollar for dollar, some amount of the money that the employee contributes, for example, 3 percent. The company typically offers a variety of stock, bond, and money market funds in which employees can invest. Money put into 401(k) plans is pretax dollars, which means that the amount you invest is subtracted from your income for tax purposes. You pay taxes on the money when you withdraw it. If you remove money from a 401(k) account before you are fifty-five years old, you must pay a 10 percent penalty in addition to taxes.

IRAs

Unlike a 401(k) plan, which is established by a company, an IRA is established by an individual. Even people who have a 401(k) plan can have an IRA. At the time of this writing, the amount you can contribute to an IRA per year is $5,000 ($6,000 for people who are fifty or older). The amount you are allowed to contribute is adjusted annually. There are two types of IRAs: traditional IRAs and Roth IRAs. In a traditional IRA, the money you contribute is subtracted from your earnings before you pay taxes. Thus, payment of taxes on that part of your income is put off, or deferred, until you withdraw the money in your IRA. This type of IRA is best for people who expect to earn less money when they retire than they will while they're working because their tax rate will be lower once they retire.

The second type of IRA is called a Roth IRA because the bill that created it was introduced into the U.S. Senate by Senator William V. Roth of Delaware. When you invest in a Roth IRA, you use money on which you have already paid taxes. However, any money you earn in the Roth IRA is nontaxable. That means you will not have to pay taxes on it when you take it out. This type of IRA is best for people who

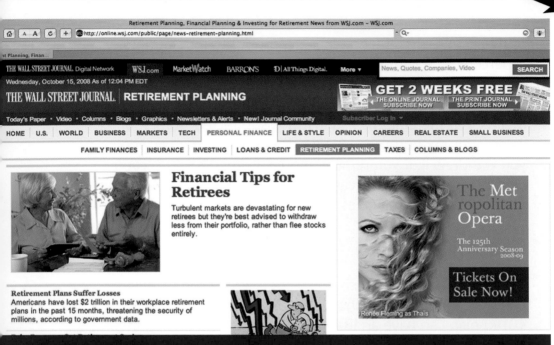

Web sites, such as this one from the *Wall Street Journal* (http://www.wsj.com), provide useful advice on investing for both general and retirement purposes and a number of automated tools.

expect to have the same or greater earnings when they reach retirement age.

Investing for Wealth

There is a second reason for investing—financial security. Having money gives you the ability to realize many of your dreams: owning a house, starting a business, working for yourself, and many other ambitions. Many people struggle to accomplish their desires on the money they earn at their jobs. The answer is to put a little money away on a regular basis. This way you can build up savings that you can use one day to do the things you want.

Educating Yourself About Investments

Today, there are at least three major cable TV channels devoted to information on financial and investment subjects: CNBC, Fox Business News, and Bloomberg TV. There are several magazines and newspapers devoted to investment news. Among the most reputable are the newspapers the *Wall Street Journal*, *Barron's*, and *Investor's Business Daily*, and magazines like *Smart Money, Money*, and *Kiplinger's*, which have helpful articles on managing your money as well as investing.

Risk and Reward

At the heart of investing is the concept of risk. You invest because you think you can make money. However, there is also the risk that you can lose the money you invest. For example, you could buy a share of stock for $10, and it could increase in value to $50 or decrease in value to $0. Some stocks are riskier than others. Often, the riskier an investment is, the greater its potential gain. However, a larger potential gain can also mean a larger potential loss. How much risk is appropriate depends primarily on the following three factors:

> **Your age:** The younger you are, the longer you have to gain back money you lose because you most likely have many working—and investing—years ahead of you.

Watching financial news channels like Bloomberg TV can keep you up to date on the events that may affect the economy and your stocks. Financial news channels offer real-time stock performance information and analysis.

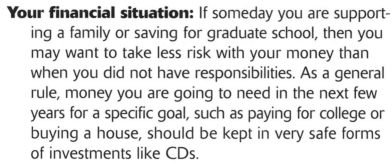

Your financial situation: If someday you are supporting a family or saving for graduate school, then you may want to take less risk with your money than when you did not have responsibilities. As a general rule, money you are going to need in the next few years for a specific goal, such as paying for college or buying a house, should be kept in very safe forms of investments like CDs.

Your personality: Some people are very adventurous. Others get nervous when they feel the money they've earned is at risk. Different people are comfortable with different amounts of risk.

The next chapter discusses your options for investing.

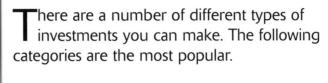

CHAPTER 4
The Basics of Investing

There are a number of different types of investments you can make. The following categories are the most popular.

Money Market Accounts

A money market account is a special type of savings account offered by some banks and investment firms. Money market accounts work in the same way as regular checking or savings accounts, but instead of lending the money from deposits, the bank uses the money to buy and sell different currencies around the world. The interest paid on money market accounts is usually higher than that paid on regular checking accounts.

Bonds

Bonds basically represent a loan to a company or government. When a company (including banks and public utilities) or government needs to raise money, it often issues bonds. When you buy a bond, you are paid interest at regular intervals,

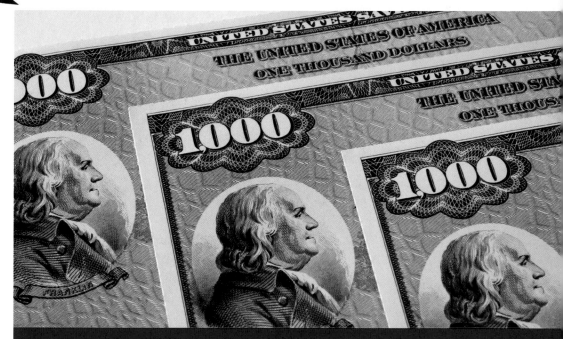

You can purchase U.S. savings bonds *(shown here)* online from the U.S. Department of the Treasury for as little as $25. When they mature, they're worth twice the purchase price.

such as monthly, quarterly (four times a year), or annually. There are several different types of bonds, including the following:

Treasury bonds: These are bonds issued by the federal government; they are available in two-, five-, and ten-year periods. These periods refer to the bonds' maturity dates (when the loan must be paid back to you).

Municipal bonds: Municipal bonds are issued by governments other than the federal government, such as states or cities. The interest earned on

many municipal bonds is not taxed as long as you
live in the state where the bond is issued.

Corporate bonds: Corporate bonds are issued by
companies. The interest rate on corporate bonds
often varies with how financially sound the company
issuing them is. Riskier companies often pay higher
interest rates than very sound companies in order
to get people to buy their bonds.

How do you know how risky a bond is? There are companies
that specialize in rating bonds. Examples of such companies are
Moody's Investors Service and Standard & Poor's. They evaluate
each company's financial state and give its bonds a rating.
For example, Standard & Poor's rates bonds from AAA to D,
with AAA being the most sound. Bonds with very low ratings
are sometimes called junk bonds. They pay a high rate of
interest but are risky because the company that issues them
may fail.

Mutual Funds

Mutual funds are a type of investment in which many people
pool their money to buy an assortment of stocks. By investing
in a mutual fund, you get to invest in a variety of companies
without having to buy shares of each one individually. Buying
shares in a mutual fund can allow you to buy shares in companies you couldn't afford to buy alone. Mutual funds are
offered by a large number of investment firms, such as Fidelity
Investments, Vanguard, and T. Rowe Price. A mutual fund is
managed by a professional who works for the company
offering the mutual fund. He or she picks the stocks that the
mutual fund contains and decides when to buy more or sell
them. Individuals buy shares in the mutual fund in the same

way they would buy shares of stock. There are many different types of mutual funds, some specializing in particular countries or industries. For a beginning investor, however, often the best choice is a diversified mutual fund, which invests in a wide range of companies in major industries. Such funds will be discussed later in this chapter.

There are two basic types of mutual funds: load and no load. "Load" refers to a percentage of the invested amount that the mutual fund company keeps as a fee when you buy shares. When the company does not charge for investing in the fund, it is said to be a "no load" fund. There are many large mutual fund companies that offer no load funds. In general, unless you are investing in a special type of fund that gives you limited choices, it is preferable to purchase no load funds. Mutual fund companies provide a booklet called a prospectus for each fund they offer. This booklet explains the investment strategy of the fund, the companies it invests in, its past performance, factors that could affect the fund, and the fees it charges. You should read the prospectus carefully before investing.

Indexes

How well is your mutual fund doing? You can find out by comparing it to an index. An index is a standard measure of the performance of the stock market as a whole. It is based on the stocks of companies on major stock markets. For example, Dow Jones & Company tracks the performance of thirty major American industrial companies and provides an average of their performance, known as the Dow Jones Industrial Average. By comparing the performance of a mutual fund to an appropriate index, you can see if the fund is performing as well as the stock market in general.

Newspapers like the *Wall Street Journal* provide listings of the daily price, performance, and other statistics for stocks, bonds, and mutual funds.

Stocks

A share of stock essentially represents a tiny share of a company. Stocks are sold in various stock markets. There are a number of different stock markets (also called stock exchanges). Two major ones are the New York Stock Exchange (NYSE) and NASDAQ (the National Association of Securities Dealers Automated Quotation system). To buy stocks, you place an order with a broker. A broker is someone who carries out transactions between buyers and sellers. There are various types of brokers. Full-service brokerage companies, such as Merrill Lynch & Co., Inc., provide investment advice and recommendations as well as processing transactions. Discount brokers, such as the Charles Schwab Corporation, place orders at a low price but provide only limited advice. Electronic brokers, such as E-Trade, allow you to place orders over the Internet. In addition, some mutual fund companies offer brokerage services, allowing you to buy stocks as well as mutual funds.

Types of Stock

There are two types of stock: common stock and preferred stock. Common stock is the type you are most likely to buy when starting out. There are two major differences between common and preferred stock. First, a company decides whether or not to pay a dividend (a percentage of the company's earnings paid to stockholders), and how much, to its common stockholders. The dividend may change from year to year, depending on how well the company is doing. Preferred stock pays a guaranteed dividend, but if a company does well and increases the dividend on the common stock, the preferred stock's dividend does not increase.

Traders are pictured here working at the New York Stock Exchange (NYSE), which is located at 11 Broad Street in New York City. Today, the NYSE operates both a physical location for the exchange and an electronic exchange.

A second difference is what happens if a company fails. If a company goes out of business, the company's remaining assets are used to pay off bondholders and stockholders. However, bondholders are paid first, then preferred stockholders, and finally common stockholders. This procedure often means that when it's time to pay common stockholders, there is no money left, and so they lose their investment.

How Stocks Earn Money

Stocks earn money in two ways. The first is by increasing in value. When a company's revenues (money it earns from sales) and profit are increasing, the value of a share of its

A variety of computerized analytical tools are available to help you decide which stocks to buy. Some allow you to "backtest" strategies to see how they would have worked.

stock increases, and people are willing to pay more for it. The difference between what you originally paid for a share of stock and its present value is called a capital gain (or capital loss, if its value goes down instead). Stocks may also pay dividends. The key to growing investments is reinvesting your capital gains and dividends. When you reinvest the money you make from investments, you buy more shares with it instead of spending it. Over time, you own more and more shares and have more and more gains and dividends.

Going It Alone vs. Using a Professional Adviser

One question that most investors ask themselves at some point is whether or not they should handle their investments by themselves or use a professional broker. The following are some of the pros and cons of using a professional broker:

Pros
The broker has more experience and is less likely to be influenced by the rumors and trends of the market.

You may feel less nervous about your choices if you have someone knowledgeable to run your choices by.

The broker may hear of new offerings you are not aware of.

Cons
If you do not have a lot of money invested with the professional broker, you may not receive much attention.

Ten Great Questions to Ask
a Professional Financial Adviser

1 What combination of investments would you recommend for someone my age?

2 What stocks would you recommend for someone my age?

3 Is it OK for me to invest in Company X?

4 Where's the best place to put money I might need in a few years when I go to college?

5 How often should I check back with you about how my investments are doing?

6 Under what conditions should I consider selling some of my stocks?

7 Under what conditions should I consider buying more stocks?

8 What bank account or money market account is paying the best interest rate right now?

9 What CDs are paying the best interest rate right now?

10 What kind of changes in my life should I let you know about so we can adjust my mix of investments?

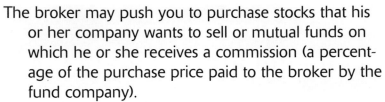
The broker may push you to purchase stocks that his
or her company wants to sell or mutual funds on
which he or she receives a commission (a percentage of the purchase price paid to the broker by the
fund company).

The broker may be more aggressive or conservative in
his or her investing than you are comfortable with.

At one time, you had only two choices: work with a full-
service broker, or invest on your own with no professional
advice. This is no longer the case. Many discount and online
brokerages, such as Charles Schwab, offer lower fees than
full-service brokers but provide access to professionals who can
advise you either free of charge or for an additional fee on an
as-needed basis.

CHAPTER 5
Principles of Sound Investing

A s you begin investing, there are a few basic principles that can help you manage risk.

Diversification

The key to protecting the money you invest is diversification. If you have all your money in stocks, and the stock market goes down, your portfolio (collection of investments) will probably decline at a rate similar to that of the market as a whole. However, if two-thirds of your money is in stocks and one-third is in bonds, then your portfolio will most likely decline less than the stock market as a whole. Putting some of your money in stocks and some of your money in bonds is an example of diversification. As an investor, you can diversify even more by putting together a combination of different categories of investments, such as stocks, bonds, CDs, and cash. You will also need to select a variety of stocks and bonds within each category. Remember that your goal is to make as much money as possible, while still protecting the money you invest.

Sectors

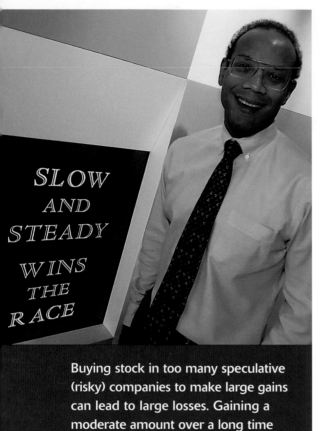

SLOW
AND
STEADY
WINS
THE
RACE

Buying stock in too many speculative (risky) companies to make large gains can lead to large losses. Gaining a moderate amount over a long time often pays off better.

Experts divide stocks into general categories based on industry. These industrial categories are called sectors. Most experts recommend that a diversified portfolio should include five to ten stocks in different industries. For instance, health care, technology, retail, and energy are all sectors. Why are sectors important? Because as various events affect the economy, companies in some sectors do well and others do worse. For example, when the economy is doing well and people's wages are going up, retail stores tend to do well. When the economy is doing poorly, companies that provide necessities like health care and food do well, but retail stores do poorly because people have less money to spend on items like clothing. It is important to make sure that the stocks you own are in different sectors because that way you will have some stocks that can do well, no matter what happens in the economy. This diversification helps protect you against large overall losses.

Sometimes, people see that one sector is hot, such as technology during the rise of the Internet, or energy as the price of oil and gas increased in 2008. They are tempted to concentrate their investments in these sectors. However, sooner or later the prospects for those industries start to look less exciting. People and institutions that invested large sums of money in those sectors cash their money out, taking profits, and the stock prices tumble. At that point, you can lose large sums of money.

How to Analyze a Stock

How do you know if a stock is good to invest in? There are a number of standard measures you can use to evaluate a stock. There are a variety of printed and online sources that provide financial information on individual stocks. Online sources include free sources like Yahoo! Finance and fee-based research resources, such as Value Line (www.valueline.com). Although the format of information provided varies from source to source, when you input the ticker symbol (one or more letters that identify a stock on a stock exchange) for a stock in an online source or look it up in a printed resource, you will see information that looks similar to this:

Fabulous Company, Inc. (FCI)

Last Trade	121.73
Net Change	-2.85
Net Change %	-2.29%
Bid	121.63
Ask	122.29
Day High	123.99
Day Low	119.67
Volume	7,155.323
52-Week High	130.93 on 07/23/2009
52-Week Low	97.04 on 01/11/2009
P/E	15

EPS	8.15
Dividend & %	2.00 (1.60%)
Capitalization	16.90B

"Last Trade" is the most recent per share price that the stock was purchased at. "Net Change" is how much the stock has gone up or down in dollars and cents. "Net Change %" is how much the stock has gone up or down as a percentage. "Bid" is the most recent amount offered for the stock. "Ask" is the most recent amount someone has offered to sell the stock for. "Day High" and "Day Low" are the highest price and lowest price, respectively, that the stock has sold for that day. "Volume" is how many shares have been traded in the last day. "52-Week High" and "Low" show the highest and lowest price the stock has traded at in the past year. The next four items are the most commonly used in evaluating a stock.

When you are considering which stock to buy, you can't just look at the price of the stock. Since companies have different levels of earnings and the price reflects what investors think the earnings will be, a stock that sells for $10 and a stock that sells for $50 may both be fairly valued if the $50 stock has much greater earnings. Instead, investors use a measure called the price-to-earnings (P/E) ratio. To get the P/E ratio, you divide the price of one share of stock by the amount of earnings per share. For example, the price of a share of stock in Fabulous Company, Inc. is $121.75, and its earnings per share are $8.15, so:

121.75 ÷ 8.15 = 14.9, which is rounded up to 15

Thus, FCI's P/E ratio is 15. Generally, the lower the number is, the better. For example, if two companies are equally promising, but one has a P/E of 10 and the other has a P/E of 15, the one

e Line – The Most Trus...

Value Line®
Welcome to The Most Trusted Name In Investment Research®

| Home | My Value Line | Education | Products & Services | About Value Line | Support | Site Map |

Welcome:
ex | My Account | Log on

scriber Portfolios Online

el Portfolios Online

e Line Resources

omic Calendar

rterly Economic Review

Value Line Industrial posite

paring the Value Line rages

Jones Long Term Chart =)

30 Value Line Reports - plimentary

Value Line Record

ks Covered in the Value Investment Survey

e Line Sample Products

nload The Value Line stment Analyzer 3.0 o

e Line Mutual Funds

cational Videos

Feeds

e Line Store

tronic Publications

tutional Services

t Publications

e Line No-Load Mutual

or More In

Hide This

"I don't know of any other system that's as good." -Warren Buffett

Today's Market Update

Midday Update with Ron Romaine

Stocks drop but interest rates rise as retail sales fall...

Continue here....

Subscriber News/Announcements

Value Line Gives Early Warning on Troubled Stocks

Value Line's Timeliness Ranking System lowered the relative price performance ranking of many of the headline-making market decliners well in advance of their recent plunge. Subscribers following our ranking system were alerted early to troubled stocks such as Lehman Brothers (rank lowered 3/31/08) and AIG (rank lowered 3/10/08)... Read More

SUBSCRIBE TODAY

THE VALUE LINE INVESTMENT SURVEY

Company Profile: Altera (ALTR)

Altera is a major provider of programmable logic devices (PLDs). PLDs are semiconductor chips that can be programmed on-site, a feature that allows customers to speed up research & development cycles and quickly bring

Value Line Viewpoint

Premium Subscriber Content

This Week's Especially Noteworthy

This week, **Provident Financial Services** makes its debut in the *Thrift Industry*, on page 1168, and **Abbott Laboratories** joins the *Drug Industry*, on page 1245...⑤Read More...

⑤ Supplementary Reports: Recent News and Analysis

▸ Jones Apparel Group - Stock Sells Off On Lowered Guidance

▸ Brink's (The) Co. - Spin Off To Conclude On October 21st

▸ Waste Management/Republic Services - Waste Management Withdraws Acquisition Bid

▸ Sovereign Bancorp - Sells Remaining Shares To Spanish Bank

Value Line (http://www.valueline.com) provides company profiles and a subscription service where you can obtain very detailed reports on specific companies.

Economic and Stock Market Commentary

▸ Stock Highlight: NATIONAL INSTRUMENTS(NATI)

▸ Getting Down to Basics - Financial Literacy 101

▸ Model Portfolio Asset Class - Emerging Market

▸ At What Price are Callable Convertibles Worth the Risk of Investment?

▸ Hedging Your Stock with Collars

Rectifier - Vishay Terminates $23-A-Share Merger Bid

▸ Gen'l Motors - Faces Sales And Liquidity Concerns; Rumors Point To Detroit Merger Talks

that has a P/E of 10 is a better value (costs less per dollar of earnings).

Earnings per share (EPS) is the amount of earnings the company generates per each share of stock that exists. The more earnings per share a company generates, the better. A dividend is a percent of profits that the company pays to stock-holders. Dividend in dollars and percent (Dividend & %) shows the current dividend that the company pays per each share of stock and the percent of earnings that the dividend represents. Not all companies issue dividends; some fast-growing companies reinvest their profits in the company to fuel its growth instead. However, among companies that do, this measure will give you an idea of how much the company pays out to shareholders, compared to other companies.

Market capitalization is the total number of outstanding shares times the price per share. Companies are divided into large cap (greater than $5 billion), midcap ($1 to 5 billion), and small cap stocks (under $1 billion). Generally, the smaller the market cap of a stock, the riskier it is.

Many company listings provide additional information as well. This information should include several years of financial information. Examining this information will allow you to see if the company is financially sound and if its revenues and earnings have been increasing on a regular basis. From the financials, you can see how fast a company is growing. The stock of a company that grows revenues and earnings faster than similar companies has a good chance of outperforming their stock. One important element is how much debt (loans) the company has. In general, less debt is better than a lot of debt. If business conditions take a downturn, companies with a lot of debt may have trouble repaying it. In addition, the report may include information on the company's business activities, its position in comparison to its competitors, and prospects for

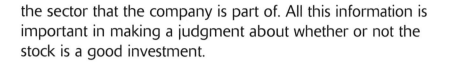

the sector that the company is part of. All this information is important in making a judgment about whether or not the stock is a good investment.

Technical Analysis

Technical analysis refers to the use of standard mathematical formulas and charts to evaluate stocks and sectors. In recent years, some brokers have developed a series of mathematical measures that track various elements of stock performance. These measures are based on theories proposed by some economists, stating that when the chart of a stock's performance conforms to certain patterns, the stock's value will go up or down. Although referring to such charts can be useful for supplementing fundamental analysis, relying on technical analysis alone can be dangerous.

Buy Low, Sell High

No matter how well you analyze stock, how many investment books you read, or how many charts you study, the ultimate behavior of stocks is never totally predictable. Unexpected events can easily cause the market to go up or down. The terrorist attacks of 9/11, the fall of the Berlin Wall, and the end of communism in Russia were all unpredictable.

The best way to protect your money, given the basic unpredictability of the market, is to buy low and sell high. The reason for this, as explained by Nassim Nicholas Taleb in his book *The Black Swan*, is that if you buy stock that is expensive and it goes down, you can lose a lot of money. Also, if you pay a lot for it, it may not go up much more. Thus, you stand to lose a lot of money if something bad happens but not gain that much if it doesn't. In contrast, if you buy a stock that's

The **NASDAQ** market site, located in Times Square, New York City, displays a ticker that shows the NASDAQ index dropped 46.26 points on that day. NASDAQ is the second-largest U.S. stock exchange and also operates eight stock exchanges in Europe.

cheap, you can't lose too much money per share if it goes down because it can only go to zero. But if your analysis is correct and it is a good company, it could potentially go up a lot and you can make money.

What does "buying low" mean? It does not mean buying stocks that cost only a few dollars. It means that you should buy stocks that are cheap in relation to their potential earnings. It means that you should buy a stock whose price is lower than you think it should be, given that the company is fundamentally sound and you think its earnings will continue to do well. Similarly, the best time to sell stocks is when they have gone up a lot. This is especially true if you are young. The market will not stay up—or down—forever. You will see many economic cycles in your lifetime. Your job is to take advantage of these cyclical changes by buying good stocks when they are cheap. Keep in mind that it's always best to buy and sell stock in increments because you have no way of knowing whether or not a stock is going to go up or down more. For example, if you want to buy 100 shares of stock, it's safest to buy it 25 shares at a time, so that you can take advantage of it going up or down further.

Investing Clubs

One excellent way to learn about investing firsthand is through an investment club. Many high schools and colleges sponsor such clubs. A teacher supervises the club. In high school clubs, students can invest either real or virtual (make-believe) money. If students use real money, the signed permission of parents or guardians is required to participate, and an adult must place the actual orders to buy and sell the stock because the students are minors. Either way, the students themselves choose the companies to invest in, perform the research on

A trader tracks the performance of a stock. The chart records the increases and decreases in the stock's price over time, helping the trader identify a good time to buy or sell.

the companies, track their stocks' performance, and make any other investment decisions.

How the Economy Affects Investments

"Economy" refers to the overall economic activity of a country. The state of the economy is measured by tracking the gross national product (GNP), the entire amount of income from all products and services provided in a year. The state of the economy affects the performance of stocks. When the GNP is growing, this means that people and companies are buying products and services in greater quantities than before. Therefore, companies are earning more. The prospect of increasing earnings tends to make the value of stocks go up.

Many things can affect the economy. One example is employment. The higher the unemployment rate, the fewer people who are working and have money to buy products and services; the reverse is true when unemployment is low. Another aspect is the availability of credit. Many businesses depend on being able to borrow money from banks to expand their businesses. When interest rates are low and credit is easily available, businesses can expand more easily and this expansion can lead to increased sales and profits.

Monitoring Your Investments

Regardless of how you keep track of your investments, it is important to review them on a regular basis. You want to evaluate each investment not only to see if it is gaining or losing money but also to consider if anything basic has changed about the company you are invested in. Some people review investments weekly or monthly. It is a good idea to review your investments at least a couple of times per year.

Myths and Facts

Myth The best way to save for a special occasion is to have the bank deduct the money automatically once each month from your account and place it in a Christmas club or other special account.

Fact The interest rate on such accounts is often lower than on a regular savings account. So, it might be better to open a regular savings account (separate from any others you have) for that purpose and make monthly deposits yourself.

Myth If a stock or sector keeps going up, it is hot and I should invest in it.

Fact Investing lots of money in hot sectors can cost you money because (1) by the time you are aware that the sector is hot, it's already had most of its gains, and (2) large investors who are all following the same trend are likely to decide to pull their money out at the same time, causing a rapid drop in those stocks.

Myth Professional brokers have inside information I don't have.

Fact Laws passed in recent years have made it illegal for corporate officers to tell brokers information that they don't share with the general public. So, all the relevant news about a company is available, if you take the time to look for it.

ask The price that someone is offering to sell a stock at.

balance The amount of money currently in an account.

bid The price that some is offering to buy a stock for.

bouncing a check Having a check presented to your bank that you don't have enough money in your account to pay.

broker A person who performs transactions between buyers and sellers.

capital gain (loss) The amount of increase (or decrease) in value of shares of stock.

commission A percentage of the sale price of an item paid to the person who sells it.

deduct Subtract from an account.

deferred Put off until a future date.

deposit Put money into.

diversified Including many different types.

dividend A share of profits paid by a company to its shareholders.

Dow Jones Industrial Average An index consisting of thirty industrial companies whose stocks' performances provide a standard measure of the stock market's value.

economic cycle A series of changes in the overall business activities in a country that occurs over and over.

exchange A company that provides facilities to trade stocks, bonds, mutual funds, or other types of investments.

increment One of a series of regular additions or contributions.

index A group of companies whose stock represents the typical performance of a market or sector.

individual retirement account (IRA) A type of investment account that provides tax advantages to encourage people to save for retirement.

interest An amount paid for the use of money.

interest rate The percentage of a sum of money paid for its use.

junk bond A bond issued by a high-risk company. Such bonds pay a high interest rate but carry an above-average danger that the company might fail.

personal digital assistant (PDA) Handheld computer, often with cell phone capability as well.

personal identification number (PIN) A series of numbers used to verify your identity.

portfolio A collection of investments.

principal The sum of money you put into an investment.

reconcile To make sure that your financial records agree with the bank's and are accurate.

return on investment The amount of money you make from an investment, in dollars or as a percentage.

virtual Make-believe.

withdrawal Money you remove from an account.

Federal Deposit Insurance Corporation (FDIC)
Consumer Response Center
2345 Grand Boulevard, Suite 100
Kansas City, MO 64108-2638
(800) 378-9581
Web site: http://www.fdic.gov
The FDIC insures bank accounts. Its Web site also provides a
    variety of information related to banking and the state of
    banks.

Fidelity Investments
82 Devonshire Street
Boston, MA 02109
(800) 544-6666
Web site: http://www.fidelity.com
The number-one U.S. provider of retirement accounts, this
    company provides information on retirement and non-
    retirement investing. Its Web site provides the latest
    news and real-time quotes.

House Financial Services Committee
2129 Rayburn House Office Building
Washington, DC 20515
(202) 225-4247
Web site: http://financialservices.house.gov
This committee is responsible for dealing with financial issues
    and bills. It is possible to view hearings over the
    Internet and obtain information on various bills that
    have been passed and are under consideration and
    their potential effects on the economy.

Investment Industry Regulatory Organization of Canada
121 King Street West, Suite 1600
Toronto, ON M5H 3T9
Canada
(416) 364-6133
Web site: http://www.iiroc.ca
This is the organization that regulates stock transactions in
    Canada and provides information about stock rules.

New York Stock Exchange
11 Wall Street
New York, NY 10005
(212) 656-3000
Web site: http://www.nyse.com/home.html
This is the most well-known stock exchange in the United
    States. Its Web site provides a variety of information
    related to stocks.

Security Investment Protection Corporation
805 Fifteenth Street NW, Suite 800
Washington, DC 20005
(202) 371-8300
Web site: http://www.sipc.org/contact.cfm
This organization insures investment accounts. It also provides
    information on protections for investment accounts.

U.S. Department of the Treasury
1500 Pennsylvania Avenue SW
Washington, DC 20220
(202) 622-2000
Web site: http://www.ustreas.gov/topics/financial-markets
The Treasury Department is responsible for monitoring and
    managing the overall state of the U.S. economy. Its Web

site includes the latest information on financial markets, as well as information on the various types of bonds issued by the federal government.

U.S. Securities and Exchange Commission
100 F Street NE
Washington, DC 20549
(202) 942-8080
Web site: http://www.sec.gov
This is the organization that regulates investing in the United States. It provides educational written publications and a variety of useful calculators on its Web site.

Vanguard
455 Devon Park Drive
Wayne, PA 19087
(877) 662-7447
Web site: http://www.vanguard.com
This is the company that pioneered the index mutual fund, which contains the same companies found in major indexes. Its Web site provides market news.

Web Sites

Due to the changing nature of Internet links, Rosen Publishing has developed an online list of Web sites related to the subject of this book. This site is updated regularly. Please use this link to access the list:

http://www.rosenlinks.com/gsm/bank

Cramer, Jim. *Stay Mad for Life: Get Rich, Stay Rich (Make Your Kids Even Richer)*. New York, NY: Simon & Schuster, 2007.

Gardner, David. *The Motley Fool Guide for Teens: 8 Steps to Having More Money Than Your Pa*. Alexandria, VA: The Motley Fool Press, 2003.

Gardner, David, and Tom Gardner. *The Motley Fool Investment Workbook*. Alexandria, VA: The Motley Fool Press, 2003.

Getty, J. Paul. *How to Be Rich*. New York, NY: Jove, 1986.

Hollander, Barbara. *Managing Money*. Chicago, IL: Heineman, 2008.

McGowan, Eileen, and Nancy Lagow Dumas. *Stock Market Smart*. Brookfield, CT: Millbrook Press, 2002.

Modu, Emmanuel, and Andrea Walker. *Mad Cash: A First-Timer's Guide to Investing $30 to $3,000*. New York, NY: Perigee Press, 2003.

Orman, Suze. *The Laws of Money, the Lessons of Life*. New York, NY: Free Press, 2003.

Tyson, Eric. *Investing for Dummies*. 5th ed. Indianapolis, IN: John Wiley, 2008.

Wuorio, Jeffrey J. *The Complete Idiot's Guide to Retirement Planning*. Indianapolis, IN: Alpha, 2007.

Cramer, Jim. *Real Money: Sane Investing in an Insane World.* New York, NY: Simon & Schuster, 2005.

Internal Revenue Service. "Retirement Plans: FAQs Regarding IRAs." Retrieved August 5, 2008 (http://www.irs.gov/retirement/article/0,,id=111413,00.html).

Kansas, Dave. *The Wall Street Journal Complete Guide to Money and Investing.* New York, NY: Three Rivers Press, 2005.

Money. "How to Make the Best of a Bad Situation." September 2008, pp. 78–84.

Morris, Virginia B., and Kenneth Morris. *Standard & Poor's Guide to Money and Investing.* New York, NY: McGraw-Hill, 2005.

Security and Exchange Commission. "Protect Your Money: Check Out Brokers and Investment Advisors." Retrieved August 5, 2008 (http://www.sec.gov/investor/brokers.htm).

Taleb, Nassim Nicholas. *The Black Swan: The Impact of the Highly Improbable.* New York, NY: Random House, 2007.

A

ATM cards, 7, 15, 17–18

B

bank, choosing a, 15–18
bank accounts, types of, 7–9
bonds, 27, 32–34, 43
bouncing a check, 19, 20
budgeting, 4–6
buying low/selling high, 49–51

C

CDs, 9, 11, 31, 43
checkbook, how to balance,
    19–22
checking accounts, 7, 8–9, 11, 12,
    17, 19, 32
checks, how to write, 12
compound interest, 9, 10–12
corporate bonds, 34

D

deposits, how to make, 12–14
direct deposit, 17
direct pay, 17
diversification, 43
dividends, 37, 40

F

Federal Deposit Insurance
    Corporation (FDIC), 11
401(k) plans, 25–27

I

identity theft, 21
indexes, 35
interest, 7–12, 19, 32–34
interest-paying checking
    accounts, 8–9
investing
    effect of economy on, 44, 53
    factors for determining risk
        level, 29–31
    for retirement, 25–28
    for wealth, 28
investing clubs, 51–53
IRAs, 25, 27–28

J

junk bonds, 34

M

minimum balance, 9, 17
money market accounts, 27, 32
municipal bonds, 33–34
mutual funds, 11, 34–35, 42

O

online account management,
    22–24

P

PIN, 15, 21, 22
professional broker, pros and cons
    of using, 40–42

R

Roth IRA, 27–28

S

savings accounts, 7–8, 11, 15, 17, 32
sectors, 44–45
Securities Investment Protection
      Corporation, 11

simple interest, 9–10
stocks, 27, 34, 35, 37–40,
      42, 43–53

T

technical analysis, 49
traditional IRA, 27
treasury bonds, 33

About the Author

Jeri Freedman has a B.A. degree from Harvard University. For fifteen years, she worked for high-technology companies, where her duties included investor relations. She has been an active investor for twenty-five years.

Photo Credits

Cover (silhouette) © www.istockphoto.com/Kristian Peetz; cover, p. 1 (top, bottom) © www.istockphoto.com/bluestocking, (middle) © www.istockphoto.com/Carolina Garcia Aranda; pp. 4–5 © Bill Aron/PhotoEdit; pp. 7, 19, 25, 32, 43 © www.istockphoto.com/Nicole S. Young; p. 8 © Michelle D. Bridwell/PhotoEdit; p. 13 © www.istockphoto.com/Jill Battaglia; p. 16 © Jim West/The Image Works; p. 20 © Phil Martin/PhotoEdit; p. 21 © www.istockphoto.com/Sean Locke; p. 26 © Mark Richards/PhotoEdit; pp. 30, 50 Mario Tama/Getty Images; p. 33 © www.istockphoto.com/Richard Cano; p. 36 © age fotostock/SuperStock; p. 38 Spencer Platt/Getty Images; p. 39 www.shutterstock.com; p. 44 © Tannen Maury/The Image Works; p. 52 © www.istockphoto.com/stevecoleccs.

Designer: Sam Zavieh; Editor: Kathy Kuhtz Campbell
Photo Researcher: Amy Feinberg